To

Row

Thanks for a
great week

Bad Boys :)

G000109965

Unconscious Incarceration

How to break out,
be free and unlock your potential

Gethin Jones

dot dot dot publishing

©2018 Gethin Jones

First Published in Great Britain 2018 by dot dot dot publishing
www.dotdotdotpublishing.com

The moral right of the author has been asserted.

All rights Reserved. No part of this publication may be reproduced, stored in a retrieval system, or transmitted, in any form or by any means without the prior written permission of the publisher, nor be circulated in any form of binding or cover other than that in which it is published and without similar condition being imposed on the subsequent purchaser.

A catalogue record for this book is available from the British Library

ISBN—978-1-907282-86-7

Design by Martyn Pentecost ©2018 mPowr Limited
DotDotDot Logo ©2018 mPowr Limited

dot dot dot publishing

edge-of-your-seat books

To
Sue Atkins
David Jones (Stewart)
Michael Sullivan

Contents

The End Begins   1

Scrooge–The Antagonist   9

Marley Moments   17

The Cabbie   27

The Tour Guide   37

Time Traveller   47

Singing Nightingale   57

The Hobblers   67

Masterful Change   79

Conclusion   89

The End Begins

Your mind is the most powerful part of you. It dictates your life and the decisions you make. You, like me and everyone else, have two sides. This is the age-old story of good versus evil. This development programme is going to show you a side of you that is hidden within, I call this your *Scrooge*.

In 1843, Charles Dickens published *A Christmas Carol*. The main character in this story of transformation was Ebenezer Scrooge. He was a miser of a man and represented all that was bad with the world at the time of its writing. In the story, Scrooge was visited by three ghosts; Christmas past, Christmas present and Christmas future. All three took Scrooge on a journey of discovery. In this book, I will introduce you to your own Scrooge, who is hidden within the shadows of your mind.

Most people are aware of the mainstream, life-destroying addictions. These are drugs, alcohol, gambling, food, sex, etc. Scrooge behaviour addictions also have the potential to destroy. Although they are subtler, they become evident in your regrets. Scrooge lives outside of your awareness. It's the behaviour that makes you repeat mistakes. You will make mistakes as everyone does. You have been blindly following your Scrooge down a dark, cobbled path.

Scrooge is invisible to us. Why? Because Scrooge is busily working within your subconscious mind. Others can see your Scrooge. They may even point him out, but he is powerful and will convince you that what they are saying is wrong. Scrooge is in control.

In this book, you have an opportunity to identify your Scrooge. You will be introduced to him by the Cabbie, the Tour Guide and the Time Traveller. These characters are similar to the ghosts that visited Scrooge on that cold winter's night in London. These characters know your Scrooge and will unveil the negative impact Scrooge is having in your life.

This book will provide you with a new way of decision-making. This new way of thinking will give you a sense of ease and freedom. It will open the door of opportunity and help you unlock your true potential. As a consequence, Scrooge will no longer be your subconscious guide.

Your eyes fly open. The room is empty, a bare shell. This familiar room resembles the pain you feel inside. There are no sheets on the bed. The duvet cover is covered in black stains. Stains from spilt ashtrays. As your mind starts to clear, it inevitably connects with the feeling of complete dread about the day ahead of you.

Your body woke up as the last traces of the heroin you injected the night before left your body, and physical withdrawal is on its way. Your nose starts running and your body shivers, oblivious to the fact that it's a warm summer's day in June. The wreck of a person that you are clambers from the bed and over to the window. There it is, the familiar sight of the train station and commuters making their way to work. Your heart sinks as a too-familiar thought enters your head. "Why can't I be like them?" They all have purpose and direction, whilst you are just a spectator. You walk back to the bed. Your head falls into your hands.

We all know those times. You want to cry, but tears don't come. The pain of your situation is there, right before you. The thought of another day is unbearable. You wish you could end it. Surely, death must be better than this! A feeling of complete hopelessness washes over you.

Your soul, if you ever had one, died many years ago. You have no connection to this world. You lost that long ago, and isolation has taken its toll. You are completely broken, there is no reason to live. But no matter how deep your torment is, there is never enough courage to end it. You truly are the living dead.

But your body jolts you back into the now, screaming for its heroin. It is the only thing that can take away the physical withdrawal. Your body sweats and shivers, and the smell of your unwashed body reaches your nose, a mixture of cigarette smoke, sweat and BO. You haven't washed for days. Your hands and nails are black from the soot. Soot from the bottom of the spoons. The spoons that you used to cook your heroin.

You go to the bathroom and glance towards the mirror. There is a pain and despair sitting in your eyes, but your mind pulls your gaze away quickly because it cannot bear looking at the reflection of the truth. There are bruises on your neck, but as you touch them there is no sensation because your nerve endings are already damaged. The bruises and numbing are from the months of injecting into the neck.

Your stomach starts to cramp and the mind switches on your obsession. What is an obsession, if not that particular thought that overrides all others? "I want a cigarette...", "I'm fat...", "I want something sweet...", "Does he/she still love me...?" Right now, the overwhelming thought, the obsession is, "I need to get some heroin."

The realisation hits your mind, solid and relentless: there is no money left and you have nothing in your flat that you can sell. There is no way of getting anything on tick. All bridges have long been burnt. You have ripped off all the local, small-time dealers. Desperation rises alongside your fear, and fear is crippling and rooting you to the spot.

Desperation is the only thing driving your mind. You drag yourself to the kitchen, and there they are, on the side the needles and spoons you used to cook up yesterday's hits. Your obsession is the only thing in the driver's seat, master of body and mind. You start gathering the spoons and filters. You used them when drawing the brown liquid from the spoon to the syringe. You decide to recook the filters, convinced that there is still enough residue to take away the withdrawal.

Your obsession is in full control, saying, "I can smell a sweet aroma rising from the spoon." You know you'll get satisfaction, and this drives you forward on the quest to satisfy your obsession. The imaginary sweet smell of heroin already fills your nose. It's the same pleasing aroma you used to get in your favourite restaurant. Your mind awakens with the expectation of your favourite delights.

There is a used needle near at hand. You rinse it under the tap and put it on top of the filter. You draw up liquid. Your heart sinks. It sinks like a dead sailor thrown overboard in his weighted hammock. There is no colour in the syringe. It is as clear as the water from the tap.

Your addicted mind takes over again. Your wreck of a body is walking. Walking back to the mirror in the bathroom. It's time to hold your breath. The vein in your neck shows itself. The needle is blunt, and it also has a barb on the point. Regardless, you push hard into the neck, forcing the blunted needle in, until it punches and tears through your skin and you drive it through the wall of the vein. Shakily, you draw back the plunger and blood enters the syringe. You then push the mixture of blood

5

and liquid back into the vein. Your mind fills with hope. Hope that relief is coming. You pull out the syringe and rest your hands on the side of the sink. Your mind is waiting. Waiting for the warmth of the substance. Waiting for the ease to your body and the mind.

Your mind is gasping for that peace. The peace you used to have when sitting in a park or garden. The feeling of warmth you used to get as the sun gently hit your skin. That feeling of calmness that arouses the inner sensation that everything is right with the world. But your peace does not come.

The realisation hits you. You have just injected water. Your heart sinks further. The dead sailor thrown overboard hits the ocean bed. Your mind drags your broken body to the front room, and your eyes take in the mess. This external mess resembles the state of your mind. Rubbish all over the floor, broken butts, spilt ashtray, dirty plates and cups.

The stale smell of the room is worse than the smell coming from your body. One chair sits among all the mess, facing the window. You sit down and your head hits your hands again, automatically. Your mind is screaming in silence, dying. The desperation to get some drugs is overwhelming. The obsession takes hold, "I need, I must, how, where, when..."

Fear, your familiar companion, is here. You connect with the fear of what you need to do to get the next hit. Your mind is torn inside, from the utter and total desperation of using. But fear of the consequences somehow roots your body to the seat.

You could steal from a shop or break into a car. You know this could lead to being arrested. Eight years of your life have been spent in prison. Your body and mind could not suffer another day of that. There is no going back to that darkness, not even for one day. But the reality of today is here, and your mind is racing. There must be some way, *some way* to get your fix. Body and mind are like a washing machine, going round and round.

What about other addicts? Are there any that you can manipulate or rip off? The message that screams back is "NO!" Your mind keeps score of all you've ripped off before. What happens if they demand the money you owe? There will be violence, but your body has no fight. There is no strength for violence.

Your wrecked body falls to its knees, eyes scanning the floor for some cigarette butts to make a roll up. There are some! It's an oasis within this dark pit. What a waste of a human life! You are but a human wreck. You stand up and walk back to the window. Your eyes stare out and find people walking by. Living a life. What you see is right there, but it might as well be a million miles away from where you're standing.

Sadness rises from the deepest crevices of your soul. You feel the dampness of a tear as it runs down your cheek. Your tears are connected to your pain. The pain of your choices past. Choices that led to so many lost dreams and missed opportunities. All of us have lost dreams and missed opportunities. Lost loves. Lost friends. Broken promises. Heartache and loneliness. They all lift up like a tsunami, overwhelming you with a wave of deep sadness. Sadness is the only thing sitting in the centre of your soul: The truth of this life is there for you to see.

This was what I call *The last day of my old way of thinking.* Although you may not be a heroin addict, you will have behaviours that you use addictively. All these habits live within your subconscious, standing just out of your awareness. You might not know that they are even there, if not for that niggling feeling that *something* is not right.

Your mind is a powerful thing that will find a myriad of ways to convince you to use these behaviours again and again. My mind was the same. Although deep inside I knew the damage the drugs were causing me, my mind would say one of two things. "*It will be different this time,*" or "*This is the last time.*" This is Scrooge at play, moving within the shadows of your mind. It is now time for you to see your Scrooge.

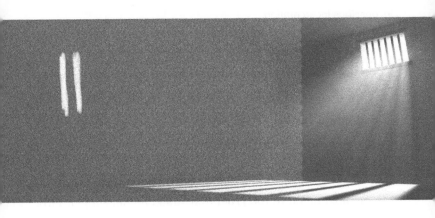

Scrooge

The Antagonist

The character Scrooge was a lost, scared and lonely man. He was trapped in a life he had built around greed. Scrooge's every moment of every day was dedicated to creating more wealth. This addictive behaviour separated him from the world around him.

Scrooge had developed a belief: his wealth was his happiness. Anyone that got in the way of an opportunity for profit was a threat to his happiness. He believed that they wanted to take away his self-made security.

In his mind, Scrooge could not see any of the damage he was doing to himself or those around him. Scrooge's desire to be a success was the veil that covered his eyes from the reality of his existence.

In the opening chapter of *A Christmas Carol*, we see how Scrooge alienated himself from the world around him. Debtors feared and avoided him, do-gooders are dismissed by him. His faithful nephew Fred, who loves him unconditionally, is rewarded with a *"Bah! Humbug!"*

On that cold Christmas Eve, Scrooge walked back to his home holding on to the gruel that would be his supper. Little did he know that he was about to go on a personal journey. This was going to be a therapeutic experience capable of pulling away the veil of denial covering his eyes.

Fear-led

Scrooge is built on fear. This part of you can be subtle or excessive, depending on your life experiences. Fear sits within the subconscious mind. This unconscious fear then drives the conscious mind. Fear leads you to the lie that believes your actions are protecting you.

Fear-led individuals will never openly trust. They are very guarded about what they give to the world. This behaviour keeps them trapped. This way of thinking stunts development and growth.

The Scrooge mindset of fear sends a message of mistrust. The fear seeps into you, creating an inability to truly engage with the world. Fear blocks true happiness, contentment and joy. Fear disconnects us from the world we live in.

Close-minded

The closed mind is based on ego. The belief that *I know best.* Like fear, this part of Scrooge also has a subtle and extreme version. Close-mindedness will get in the way of personal growth. Scrooge believes that the world is wrong. Only Scrooge is right. So he/she will dismiss any ideas that may be given to him/her.

Close-mindedness blocks all learning. This includes emotional, professional and intellectual development. However, you need to know that to stop is to move back. The rest of the world is always moving forward. It moves forward with or without us. You can see the close-minded part of you when you are speaking with someone. If you pay close attention to your mind, you may discover that you are dismissing what they are saying. Scrooge is only considering what is going to be said next, and the natural Scrooge response will be to shut down any idea or suggestion.

Close-minded people frustrate those around them. People will leave the conversation with the sense they've wasted energy and time. Scrooge will dismiss all everyone else says and carry on, regardless. The close-minded behaviour is rooted in an attitude of superiority. This keeps the mind shut tight.

Denial

Denial is what blinds you from identifying your personal Scrooge. It can be a coping mechanism, especially for someone who has suffered great trauma. This is also portrayed in Scrooge's story. Denial can be broken down to the phrase "Don't even know I am lying." (This is about lying to self, rather than to others.)

Denial of behaviours leads to blaming others. "It's everyone else's problem", "I don't need to change," "Everyone else needs to change." Denial is the number one behaviour that needs to be confronted because it will prevent any change from happening.

Denial is the proverbial *head in the sand*. It's the inability to see the truth. This behaviour will also lead to a complete disregard for anyone else's point of view. Denial maintains the fundamental belief that you are right. It is everyone else who is wrong. A person in denial will make believable excuses. Scrooge reasoning will justify the excuses.

Judging/Judgement

Judging/judgement is a form of defence. Everyone you meet is immediately judged. This behaviour is part of the primal safety response: Fight or flight. However, there is a difference between this and Scrooge's judging/judgement. The Scrooge version will judge and look down. The looking down behaviour will dismiss anything else others may have to offer. This is closely linked to Scrooge's close-mindedness and fear. Scrooge has separated you from the world around you.

When judging, you are looking out, not in. You are continuing to create the belief that you know best. "I don't need help." You believe that no one else can do anything for you. Judging reaffirms that you are OK. The judgement belief can say, "They are below me, and they know nothing. I am a better person than them. They just want something." These responses are also linked to fear and ego.

Judging leads to a feeling of being superior (ego), the feeling of being better than those around you. This is also called the inflated ego. An inflated ego is evident in the workplace. For instance, one worker will disregard the work being done by other colleagues. Or a worker will also show lack of respect for the boss. People trapped in this Scrooge behaviour will believe that they are the lynchpin of their organisation. Everyone else in their particular world should be as they are.

Greed

In the original story, Scrooge's greed was based on money. Having more money brought about a feeling of safety and security that said, "I'm OK." The greedy part of you is not just about money or possessions. Greed can relate to other things, like withholding of emotion, time and support. Greed says, "If I am not getting, then I am not giving. Why should I give? What's in it for me?" This behaviour is ugly and will inevitably lead to people avoiding you.

However, the safety and security sought through greed are lies. Greed leads to a deep feeling of loneliness, and this loneliness hides behind a wall of denial. And denial only says, "I am OK". In Dickens' *A Christmas Carol*, Scrooge's denial created isolation and loneliness. Greed is like grasping sand with your hands. No matter how hard you clench it, sand will always fall through your fingers, leaving you with nothing.

Lonely

Loneliness is another part of you that sits within the subconscious. The conscious mind will not want to admit to the existence of loneliness. You may have a family, a team or a business. You may be invited to events and celebrations. The Scrooge part of you is that old feeling of being personally disconnected.

When you identify your Scrooge, you will see that you are not truly connected. You are *lonely within a crowd*, emotionally disconnected from the world around you. This loneliness is driven by all the other parts of your Scrooge behaviours (greed, judgement and being close-minded.) No one wants to admit to being lonely. Scrooge would never admit being lonely. He has all he needs!

Isolated

Scrooge behaviours will isolate you. This is achieved both subconsciously and consciously. At the subconscious level, you are reacting through Scrooge behaviours. Scrooge will actively work to separate you from the world around you.

Within the conscious, the person sees being isolated as a positive thing. They justify it by saying, "I'm more productive.

Others get in the way. I can take care ⟨
the constant interference of others." ⟨
denial that steers the subconscious

Human beings are social. This
developed. Isolating yourself from the ..
humanity. Humans need to be part of the collective becau⟨
that is how we learn, develop and evolve together. Pursuing
isolation breeds resentment and fear. However, Scrooge says,
"No one is of any benefit to me."

Imprisoned

Scrooge entraps you in addictive behaviours, and these
behaviours imprison you inside your subconscious mind. Being
trapped by this part of you is a disaster. You will eventually
sentence yourself to a lifetime of misery that you cannot
escape, a misery that sits within the mind.

Scrooge has imprisoned you in a way of thinking and being
that isolates you and sentences you to a lifetime of *repeated
patterns*. These patterns can be constant in a number of areas,
such as business failure, job losses, relationship break-ups,
arguments with family, friends or colleagues.

The imprisoned mind's walls are made of bricks. All the
Scrooge traits I mentioned earlier are the bricks of that wall.
This wall, denial, is what kept Scrooge and myself trapped.
Without awareness, there was no release date in sight.

...was in that flat my Scrooge was there for all to see. ...e but me. I was selfish and only considered myself. I had ...e ego that said, "I can beat my dependency." I felt I didn't ...ed any help from anyone. I also never trusted or believed in anything that anyone said. I was completely close-minded. I would ask for help, only to dismiss the help or suggestions I was offered.

However, that day strange things were happening in my mind. As I stood by that window, I remember tears running down my cheeks. The walls of denial were being breached. I could see the wreck of a man I had become. As I stared blankly out the window, I could see my reflection looking back. I was face-to-face with my Scrooge. The selfishness and self-centeredness that was at my core. The close-mindedness preventing me from growing and developing. The anger and resentment towards the world around me that were eating me alive. I was filled with jealousy of others and self-pity. My Scrooge was in control, dictating the choices and decisions I made. And it was these decisions that had delivered me into the world of the damned.

Marley Moments

Marley moments are thoughts, feeling or comments suggesting that something is not quite right. Marley lives within your mind, swimming between the conscious and subconscious. Marley moments resemble the character of Jacob Marley in the story of Scrooge.

Scrooge got to his front door and turned the key in the lock. As he did, the knocker morphed into the face of his dead business partner, Jacob Marley. Jacob Marley's face was wild with flyaway hair. His eyes wide open and motionless, with the most horrible, livid colour. Scrooge shivered at this sight, shaking his head as he entered his home.

Jacob Marley was a spirit, whereas Scrooge was still alive. Jacob was paying for the sins of his life. This meant he would be living for eternity in chains. Jacob Marley wanted to give Scrooge a chance to escape such a fate. It was time to give Scrooge the opportunity to see the error of his ways. Only by recognising this and changing would he be able to save himself from his subconscious chains.

Jacob was the voice inside, saying, "Something must change."

At first, Scrooge tried to ignore this voice. When Jacob materialised, Scrooge refused to believe in him and blamed indigestion instead. At this response, Jacob raised a frightful cry and shook his chains with such a noise that Scrooge held on tight to his chair.

Jacob Marley then explained that Scrooge was going to be introduced to three spirits, the ghosts of Christmas Past, Christmas Present and Christmas Future. These spirits were to take Scrooge on a journey that would dismantle the wall of denial and show him the truth of his existence.

The Truth

The truth is all around us. It sits within, but is hidden. It's hidden by the world we have built around us. We have built our thoughts on information provided by Scrooge. Marley is the deliverer of the truth.

Marley's job is to connect you to the truth. When this happens, it will set off feelings and thoughts that suggest all is not as it is meant to be. Marley is within us all. He will also connect you to other people who can help. I call them *the Singing Nightingales*. They are insightful as they see the truth that lives within you. Personal denial stops you from seeing the truth within.

The truth is the key and Marley leads you to the key. This key will open the door to your denial. However, unlocking the door is only the first step. Once connected to the truth, you have to start smashing your denial. As you do this, Scrooge will be exposed and, once exposed, you can start saying, "Scrooge no more."

Change Maker

Marley is the change maker, the one that starts the process of change. Before change occurs, you need to know why. As Marley swims around the mind, he will be showing you the why. You need to connect to the why so the change process can be started.

Marley wants to move you from the subconscious to the conscious mind. Change can only happen when we start to see the truth of what is. Marley can see the truth. He is not connected to any one area. Marley is the observer of the mind.

Marley will swim between your thoughts, feelings and memories. Marley cannot be contaminated by the stories we tell ourselves. Stories are created in the mind. They are fuelled by doubt, disbelief and fear. Marley's gift is being able to see the truth. Marley then sends messages from the subconscious into the conscious.

Doorman

Marley is a doorman who needs to take ownership of the key. Although the key is easily seen by Marley, it is not easy to reach because it is buried deep within the subconscious mind. Marley must swim deep into the caverns and crevices of the subconscious. These are the dark places within the workings of your mind.

When Marley reaches the key, it won't always budge. It is locked within the denial brick wall you have built. Marley breaks this down brick by brick. It's only then that Marley can grasp your key. Marley uses the key to unlock the door to the conscious mind. This key has the power to unlock the parts of you that Scrooge has been hiding. The key will show you your true self.

Swimming back to the conscious mind is never easy. The mind is a matrix and the route taken down will no longer exist. The routes have been closed by fear, doubt and disbelief. This is the mind's way of resisting change. Marley will never give in to them and will send messages that will create new pathways to the conscious. Once in the conscious mind, Marley will put the key into the lock.

Slum Clearing

Slum clearing starts to happen when the key is turned. The door of denial can be blocked by the slums of the mind. When this happens, Marley will become stronger and will deliver thoughts and feelings indicating that things are not right. This will be when the subconscious starts to become conscious.

At this point, Marley finds connections to the human voice of the Singing Nightingales. You will then start to share that something is not right. You will start to search for the solution. This is the first conscious step that will bring the change you need. However, not everyone wants to leave the slums. It is easier for you to retreat back to the slums. You return with the belief that nothing needs to change. If you return, Marley will become even louder. He will be swimming faster and faster. Creating a drowning noise that screams "Something needs to change."

Marley can also be the slum clearer for others. Marley can see the Scrooge in all of those around you. This could be at work, with family or friends. He will be challenging their Scrooge by telling the truth–*Tough Love*. Marley knows that, by doing this, he can jeopardise his relationship. However, Marley is compelled to do so. As Marley understands the truth and wants to help, others find peace and success.

Inner Love

Marley is connected to your inner self. Your inner self is filled with love for you. Deep within we all have compassion for ourselves. Changes that are identified will be uncomfortable and at times painful. You will be unclear of why you need to go through such hardship whilst changing. When this happens, you will resist. Marley will connect you to the inner love. Change is about taking care of self.

When Marley connects to the inner love, he can see your potential. Marley can look past the pain and see the happiness and joy that will come after change. Marley is your inner love and will give subconscious love to you. Marley will constantly be reassuring you that what you are doing is right.

Marley is always in battle with your doubt, your disbelief and fear. These thoughts are what will be pulling you back. Marley works hard, sending constant messages to counteract this negative part of your mind. Marley is the subconscious example of love overcoming hate. The battle that sits within everyone.

Soul Fixer

In *A Christmas Carol*, Marley was Scrooge's soul fixer. In the original story, Marley was living an eternity in chains. Even though he was dead, Marley was filled with compassion and love for Scrooge. Marley came back to Scrooge because he wanted to save his friend's soul. Marley was guiding him away from the future that lay before him.

As the soul fixer, Marley must connect us to the pain we cause ourselves. Remember, Marley is not real. You can't touch or see him. He is a part of you that no one else can see. He is your past, present and future. Marley will soon be introducing you to three characters. *The Cabbie*, who will take you back; *The*

Tour Guide, who will show you what is; and then, finally, *The Time Traveller*, who will show you what could be.

Marley was there at your birth and watched your soul grow. He witnessed you develop through childhood. Marley would have seen how the soul was chipped away. In some cases, it may have been almost completely ripped out. But Marley will be looking at how to fix your soul. Marley will place the responsibility on your conscious, true self. It is your responsibility to repair and take care of the soul because your soul is what gives meaning and purpose to your life.

Pathfinder

Marley created the pathway that led to Scrooge's complete transformation. Being a pathfinder is one of Marley's main roles. As Marley swims around the workings of the mind, he creates links between the conscious and unconscious mind. These paths will lead to successful changes.

Marley understands the purpose of change and will lead you through each of its stages. He will introduce each element leading to your personal development. Your mind is a complex maze, full of trapdoors and dead ends. Without the pathfinder, you will fall into confusion and uncertainty. Without the pathfinder, you will repeat your Scrooge behaviours.

Marley knows the beginning and the end. Marley will introduce the characters that will build the path to successful change because he knows the experts that live in your mind. These characters will take you on a journey to what was, what is and what could be. Marley and his companions will only give you what you can handle. Too much, too soon will lead to you veering off the path. Wrong turns will make the process longer and harder than it needs to be.

Selfless

Your Marley is as completely selfless as the Marley in Dickens' story. Marley was leading Scrooge to redemption. Without Marley, Scrooge's fate was sealed. He would be wandering in chains for all eternity. The Marley of the mind is the same. He swims around the mind as a separate entity. Marley belongs nowhere within the mind, body or soul.

The selfless actions are not based on want, greed or thanks. Marley only wants what is best for your true self. Marley only wants to translate what goes on in your mind. He does this so you can be successful personally and professionally. Marley understands that personal and professional success will lead to freedom and happiness.

Marley will keep swimming for the rest of your life, always looking for the next change. Marley's only purpose is to serve you and deliver you happiness. Marley knows that although your mind is your greatest gift, it can also be your worst enemy. An enemy that will imprison you. Marley helps you make sense of the mind. Marley's purpose is to deliver the freedom of what is possible. Marley will then guide you to embrace change.

With the heroin withdrawal getting stronger, you feel trapped. You are motionless as you stare out of the window, taking in the world outside. And right there, as you stand in front of the window, you become aware of Marley. Marley had been swimming around the subconscious mind, sending messages that something was not quite right.

Marley was swimming faster than ever before. The thoughts, feelings and messages were becoming a deafening drum. Marley was delivering the message that change needed to happen. Denying this change would lead to further destruction of who you are. He knew that you were heading to more of the same. *If nothing changes, then nothing changes.*

Marley was swimming furiously. He was connecting the thoughts, feelings and comments that you had been denying. Marley was about to take you on a journey. This journey would allow you to create a brand-new way of thinking.

Marley was hard at work in your subconscious. He had been swimming for weeks. You know this as every day you woke up with the thoughts, "Is this it? Is there nothing else? What is life about? There must be more?" These questions all came from Marley. His swimming around your subconscious leaves you contemplating your life.

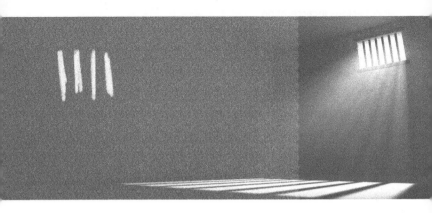

The Cabbie

The Cabbie is the next part of the personal development process. Within any change process, we need to connect with where we have come from. The Cabbie is my representation of the Ghost of Christmas Past that Scrooge met on that cold Christmas Eve.

As the clock bell struck one, Scrooge felt a presence in his room. Opening the bed curtains, he came face to face with the spirit of Christmas Past. Scrooge took his arm, and they flew off into the night. The ghost was taking Scrooge on a journey into his past so he could connect with the memories of what was and see the decisions he had made.

The Ghost of Christmas Past gave Scrooge the opportunity to re-live the images he was seeing. The sadness, the happiness and the regret. Scrooge felt the regret as watched his younger self let go of his girlfriend, Belle. He knew that this had been caused by his greed. Scrooge shouted at his younger self, "Do not let her go."

Scrooge always thought, *Bah! Humbug!* of Christmas. But during his time with the Ghost of Christmas Past, he could see that he had once enjoyed this festive time of year. He watched himself dancing at the party set up by his first boss, Mr Fezziwig. Mr Fezziwig was everything Scrooge was not: kind, compassionate and selfless.

Memories

The Victorian cabbie works with Marley. The cabbie drives around the brain that holds the memories of what was. The cabbie knows these cobbled streets well. The cabbie will start the process of opening the door further. Memories are a vast expanse that sits within the mind. This is why we need the cabbie.

The cab driver has the knowledge of the mind. Like the real cabbies, he knows the dark streets of London's Whitechapel. He knows every road, street, avenue and mews. The cabbie will get every passenger to their destination.

The mind is full of memories that can distract the real self. These memories will want you to pop down the happy memories that convince you all is OK. Scrooge will tempt you to go there because he does not want you to visit the memories that live within your slums. Scrooge knows these memories invite change. This scares Scrooge. He is at risk.

Your cabbie is aware of the distracting memories. He will avoid these and take you to your true destination. The cabbie will remind you of the places you have been. The people you have met and the decisions you have made. Whilst within these memories, you will be taking sections of them with you. The memories that will start to create the true picture of what was.

Fisherman

The cabbie is an expert fisherman. The fishermen on the Thames are very wise. They only keep fish that are useful. They throw back those that are of no use. The cabbie has the same wisdom. He will be hooking you into your memories. But, like the fisherman, he will only keep the memories that matter. The cabbie will discard those that have no meaning.

Not all memories are useful, and some may not be real. Some memories will be made up of stories you have told yourself. These then become falsehoods. The cabbie will ignore them and connect you to your self-honesty.

The cabbie helps you identify the memories that have meaning. He is the expert in knowing what fish to hook. The Ghost of Christmas Past in the original story of *A Christmas Carol* was the same. The cabbie takes you to the destinations where fish are large and easily seen so that they can be hooked. The fish are caught, and memories are highlighted. It is at this point that the learning can then begin.

29

Shadows

The cab driver is your guide, and he will guide you. He begins by asking, "Who is there? What do you see? How does it feel?" These questions lead to the shadows. The shadows of your memories are taking shape. You can start to connect with who you once were, connecting to the memories that led to who you are and the decisions you have made.

The shadows are shadows because you have hidden them well. It will take courage to ask the questions and bring the shadow into the light. Once in the light, you can see how things really were. These memories becoming more vivid will start the journey to the conscious. Once there, you will start to see the parts that need to be laid to rest. Laying to rest is acknowledging your past as a learning experience. These memories are relevant but not needed today.

Hindsight

Whilst in the cab, you will talk to the driver about what you have seen. You will start the "if only" conversation. Scrooge did this when seeing Belle. He shouted at his younger self to follow Belle. Scrooge did this because he had the gift of hindsight (yesterday into today).

You may think that hindsight is not that useful, but it is. The cabbie will explain the power of hindsight. The cabbie explains that in the *now* you can pause at any time. You look at the decisions you are making and ask, "Is this pattern like a pattern within my memories?" This is how you can learn from hindsight.

The cabbie has given you an understanding of how to use hindsight. With this understanding, you can reduce the risk of repeating poor decisions. You can also use this in a positive way. You can say that "Following this pattern has been useful in the past." Using your hindsight can lead to more positive experiences happening in your life today.

Truth

The cabbie is the owner of the truth that sits within your memories. The cabbie delivers you to your memories. There you will be confronted by the truth. What truth? The truth of who you truly are and the decisions you have made. There is the saying, "The truth will set you free." The truth will take down the wall of denial and enable change.

The cabbie will be asking questions that will take you deeper into your memories. He is taking you on a journey, and every journey needs to have purpose. The purpose of this journey is to understand your past experiences. Why take this cab ride if you are not ready to learn? This is your opportunity to understand the memories of yesterday. Are you willing or unwilling to see or understand the truth?

The cabbie will explain how difficult it is to acknowledge your own truth. He will also explain that without the truth you are in the land of make-believe. Within the land of truth, you will be able to make a factual decision. The awareness of truth will lead to meaningful changes.

Inner Self

To understand the truth, you need to connect with your inner self. We all keep this well-hidden. The inner self is well-protected, as this is where we are most vulnerable. It is the part that we don't like anyone to see and is masked by ego. The conscious mind will always be looking to protect our inner self. This is why people can either have none or very few intimate relationships. Intimacy can be broken down to "*Into me you see.*"

The cabbie steers the horse-drawn carriage that takes us to that inner self. It's the inner self that drives the decisions we make. The cabbie is asking, "Why not show your real self? What stops you? What is holding you back? What are you scared of?"

When visiting memories, you will explore the decisions you have made. You will start to question why you made them. Were you true to yourself? Or were you protecting that vulnerable inner self? The cabbie will be delicately manoeuvring you around the memories. He must do this as the unconscious inner self can connect to the conscious mind with lightning speed. If connected, the cabbie will be pulled out of the unconscious mind.

Inner Wisdom

Wisdom is a gift that is within us all. The cabbie is the vehicle that can shine a light on your inner wisdom. The cabbie translates the information stored within your memories. Inner wisdom comes from the experiences of your life. These experiences can become your wisdom, but only once you have learnt from the experiences you've had.

As the cabbie drives around your memories, you are speaking with him. The conversations you are having in the cart will open your inner wisdom. What happened there? What else could you have done? What would you change? This inner wisdom is what will take you forward.

The cabbie has asked questions and shown you what was. You are now taking this into the conscious mind. Once there, you will reflect on the lessons you have learnt. It will then be time to share these with the people you trust in your life.

Reality Maker

This reality of what once was is now clear in your mind. The cabbie has done his job, he has initiated the second stage of change. The cabbie has linked the subconscious to the conscious. The cabbie has taken your true self into the memories of your past. Now you see the reality of what truly was. No more excuses or blaming others. It's now time to take ownership of your past and your decisions. Accepting this truth helps you see how this impacts today.

In *A Christmas Carol,* Scrooge identified happiness, joy, loneliness and loss. This was the reality of his past. The reality maker is a gift; it is a window. A window that appears within the brick wall of your denial. Looking through the pane of glass you can see the truth of what once was.

The cabbie will now leave the conscious mind. At that point, you will be introduced to the tour guide. The cabbie will remain sitting in the corner of your mind, waiting. He will be there when you next need to visit the memories of yesterday.

You move away from the window and fall into the armchair. The familiar seat is a mixture of ash stains, fag burns and the stench of damp and sweat. The smell rises through your nostrils and makes your insides squirm. Leaning forward, your head falls back into your hands. That empty feeling of hopelessness rises from the pit of your stomach. The same feeling that has been haunting your mind every day, for weeks.

Marley was connecting the broken soul to the cabbie. The cabbie had the knowledge of the past memories. The cabbie was getting ready for the journey to the darkest recesses of the mind. He was going to reconnect the memories of what once was. Marley shouted, "Taxi for Scrooge."

Sitting in that stinking armchair the mind starts to revisit the past. The people you had met and the decisions that had been made. It was time to see the choices of this life. This was the moment for the true self to witness the growth of the Scrooge within.

How many lost opportunities there had been... Partners that walked away, the neglected friendships that slipped away, the jobs that were never applied for, the house that was never owned. Staying in a life of unfulfilled dreams.

Every negative decision led to this feeling of regret. The regret connected to a deep feeling of sadness. This sadness is hidden from the world, but it was there to see every time your eyes connected in the mirror. The eyes never lie, they tell the whole story of what really was. All those decisions were dictated by the subconscious. Those choice were masterly constructed by the Scrooge within.

The cabbie is showing you what really was. There is the realisation that it was you who allowed your Scrooge to grow.

This way of decision-making got you to this pitiful place you now call your life. The realisation is sitting within the conscious mind. It is in this part of the mind that you can retake control. Awareness prevents you from being controlled by Scrooge.

Sitting on that chair, you feel the dampness on your cheeks. The tears have been flowing freely from the eyes. The tears are the physical release. Your mind was connected to the memories of your past, and you can now see the shadows of your former self.

The Tour Guide

The power of the now is the most important part of change. It is only in the here and now that any change can occur. The tour guide is the one that will show you what really is. He will show you images that will challenge the truth that has been created behind your veil of denial.

The bell strikes two, and there is a bright light coming from under the door. Scrooge opens the door, and the light makes his eyes squint. There, before him is the Ghost of Christmas Present. The tour guide and Ghost of Christmas Present serve the same purpose. They pull Scrooge from the shadows and into the light of today.

The Ghost of Christmas Past takes Scrooge to the home of Bob Cratchit. Bob is Scrooge's faithful employee, who is paid a pittance for the work he delivers for Scrooge. The poverty of Bob's life is before Scrooge's eyes, and he sees Tiny Tim for the first time. Tiny Tim is Bob's son, a disabled little boy. Because of the poor wages he receives from Scrooge, Bob is unable to pay for the medical care that Tim needs.

Even so, Bob still feels gratitude for the job Scrooge gives him and raises a toast of thanks. It is a thanks for the small bounty that will be their minimal Christmas. Bob's wife is reluctant to raise her glass but does, not for the love of Scrooge but for the love of her husband.

The Ghost of Christmas Past is connecting Scrooge with the reality that his actions are having on himself and those around him. Scrooge does not like being in this place. Scrooge does not want to see the consequences of his actions.

Heart

The tour guide is connected to both the heart and mind. The tour guide knows that the heart and mind can act in different ways. Both the heart and mind can drive the decisions you make. A decision made from the heart is based on feeling. This kind of decision is one that can lead to upset.

Sometimes managers employ someone because they like who they are. Soon after, they may realise that they are not the person they thought they were. Then they struggle to let them go for fear of upsetting them.

On the other hand, decisions from the mind can lead to the opposite side of the spectrum. Being too methodical in your thinking and decision-making can disconnect you from being human. Scrooge was disconnected from his loyal employee Bob Cratchit. The job of the tour guide is to connect head *and* heart.

Vision

The tour guide will take you into the reality of your *today*. Whilst travelling around, the tour guide will be translating what he sees. The tour guide will be showing all that is, allowing you to see the world in which you live.

The tour guide will give you a vision of the reality of what is. The fictional story (denial) created in your mind will be exposed. People interpret their reality in a way that meets their vision. This is the rose-tinted-glasses scenario; people see what they want and believe this to be true. Looking deeper, you can see that this story can be fictional.

Some people create this story into a believable reality that justifies their today. The tour guide's vision is an opportunity for you to be honest with yourself. When being truly honest, you can look through the window. This was the window that appeared in your wall of denial.

When Scrooge was visited by the Ghost of Christmas Present, he was taken to his nephew Fred's house. Scrooge then saw the truth rather than the fictional story he had created for himself. He then connected to the truth of the decisions he had made. At this point, you start reflecting on the memories you collected whilst with the cabbie. As you reflect, you see how past decisions have led to where you are today. The time traveller's vision is allowing you to see your true self.

The Living

Your reality has now become clear. You start to recognise the changes that may need to take place. Marley has brought the thought, feeling or idea that something is not right. Thanks to the cabbie this is now very much within your conscious mind. The tour guide is now showing you what really is. He is starting to ask the questions. "Are you happy with this? Are you ready to consider changing something?"

The here and now is the only place where true change can happen. The tour guide brings you into the here and now. The tour guide knows that this is the place where you need to be. Your mind has a way of thinking about the past or thoughts of what tomorrow could bring. This avoids noticing what truly is.

When you are with the tour guide, you need to stay present. Focusing on the now and how you feel about your life today. It might be that you are happy with parts of your life. You may also see that you are not truly happy with other parts. Then you will look at the decisions you've made. Is your Scrooge at play? What you could change?

Joy

There is joy all around us. It's our choice if we want to connect to this joy too. It is you who chooses whether to have a life filled with joy or not. The tour guide will be showing you the joy that is in plain sight. The joy is in the smiles of those around you.

It's on the faces of the children playing hoop on the cobbled streets. How much joy do you feel in your life?

As the tour guide shows you all the areas of your life today he asks, "Are you experiencing all the joy that is available to you? Does your life lack joy? Are you happy and progressing both personally or professionally?" The tour guide's voice will be getting louder. He is asking... "Do you want to start making new decisions and choices? Or are you willing to remain on the current path?"

Loss

Loss can take many shapes. It can be related to all areas of our lives. A loss could be personal (friends, relationships, family) or professional (jobs, promotions, the collapse of a business). It can also even be opportunities (not buying that house, not going on that holiday, not investing in that deal). Two things are happening whilst with the tour guide. You are experiencing the here and now and connecting to the memories you visited with the cabbie.

The tour guide understands the workings of your mind. He understands how the Scrooge in you has affected who you are today. When the tour guide connects to your loss, he will be asking, "What could have been?" Connecting to thoughts of what-was and could-have-been is a great driver of change. Loss can reignite the passion that may have become dormant. The tour guide is connecting the heart and mind.

Choices

The tour guide's main objective is to bring you choice. Whilst with the tour guide you hear his soft voice saying... "Is this what you want? Are you happy with your lot? What could you change?"

The questions related to choice will be going deep into your mind; the burning knowledge that all is not right. At this point, your Scrooge will have been exposed. You will understand the message from Marley, the cabbie and the tour guide. Their message is *choice*. Is it now time to change or do you want to stay the same?

Self-Questioning (Am I OK?)

The questions of choice are now at the forefront of your mind. The three guides have started the internal questioning of self. That age-old question of *who am I?* This question becomes more real, and only you can answer the question. The guides' only purpose is to facilitate an environment of change. Your inner self can start the journey to find out who you truly are.

Without a question, there is no answer. If you never question yourself, you will continue creating more of the same. The question is just the question. The answer will come from within you. You now have the tour guide's version of what is. You also have the understanding of the cabbie's visit to your past truths. These elements will ignite the question. Are you ready to seek the answer?

Suddenly, you're jolted back to reality with cramping in the stomach. Pain doubles you over. The tight twisting sensation makes you grimace. This is withdrawal kicking in, literally. Your whole body is damp with sweat and every muscle is starting to ache.

It is 9 am. You can go and get your daily dose of methadone from the chemist. The chemist is a twenty-minute walk away. The thought of the walk is unbearable. It is like being at the foot of Mount Everest, staring at the summit that is out of reach.

The need for relief pushes you to your feet. You walk vampire-like out of the flat into the daylight. Your eyes squint as the blazing sun hits the eyes. The heat is unbearable. Your body sweats and shivers as withdrawal takes hold.

You are walking the streets of the city where you have lived your whole life. The tour guide is showing you all that you are and all that is going on around you. You hear a car beep. Fear rises and you panic, mind racing. Is this someone you have ripped off or owe money to?

Calmness returns as you see Mattie waving. He was a school friend, his smile big on his face. What has he got that you have not? In your mind, you hear the faint voice of the tour guide. "Mattie has a life." A life like Mattie's is something that you have always yearned for. Why couldn't you have a life like his? You know why... Scrooge was your master; the master of your personal destruction.

In the distance, you hear children playing. It's the local primary school, and the children are out on the playground, playing their games; a whirlwind of laughter and singing. As you get to the fence, the tour guide makes you stop and your eyes take in the sight of the children playing and smiling in the sunshine. You see girls playing together with a long skipping rope. Two girls are swinging the rope and another girl is jumping. They are all singing a tune to the rhythm of the rope. You can also see some boys running in between the other children as they play chase. They are laughing and shouting to their friends as they avoid being caught.

Seeing the children in the school makes you think of your son. He is nine years old and will be in a playground too. You wonder if he is playing chase with his friends. Is he thinking of you? You again hear the tour guide's voice, "Why would he think of you? What have you actually done for him?"

The tears return. You stop and lean against a garden wall. You face the wall with your hands pressed against it. You can feel the coolness of the brickwork and the crumbling cement on your palms. Your face is hidden as you don't want people to see the tears that are now streaming down your face.

The feeling of sadness is absorbing every inch of you. It is a deep chasm of loss and regret. You can't see any light, just darkness. You can see that the world around you is full of life. You are just an observer of what really is. Deep within the mind is a question that is like a splinter in your mind. It's the voice of the tour guide, "The vision you see is the living. Are you truly living?" The question and the answer are too big to acknowledge. You turn your gaze and look to the floor and continue walking.

You look up and discover you have reached your summit. The chemist door stands before you. As you push the door open, you feel the gentle relief of the cold air from the air conditioning. The cool, crisp air reacts to the sweat on your brow. It is a welcome relief from the burning heat. Every step felt like you were trudging through the deep, wet mud of a river bed.

You walk to the counter and the lady looks up and smiles. She says, "One minute, Gethin. The pharmacist is just doing the methadone prescriptions now." You take a seat and start to take in the surroundings. Your eyes see the order and tidiness of the shop. The shop has that familiar smell of all chemists. The mixture of sterilised medicines with perfumes from the toiletries.

You watch customers come in and buy goods and collect prescriptions. You can hear the faint mumble of voices but can't make out what is being said. The mind is just thinking of the thick green liquid you will be getting. You know it will take away this physical pain and fill you with artificial energy.

"Gethin," it's the voice of the pharmacist. She has the 50ml bottle of green sweetness. The lid is off. You must drink it in front of her. You take it from her softly saying, "Thank you." You make no eye contact, you can't look at anyone. You drink the liquid and feel the familiar thickness as it slides down your throat. The taste is unlike any other medicine. It is neither nice nor bad, it is both sweet and bitter.

The methadone sends a message to the mind. It's a faint light in the darkness of the day. You put the bottle on the counter and mutter another "Thank you." You turn and walk towards the door and you hear her say, "See you tomorrow, Gethin. Have a nice day." You raise your hand and leave.

As you open the door and leave the shop, you pause as the heat hits you. It's like the wall of heat that you hits you when you step off a plane on holiday. You start to walk the 100 yards to some steps. The steps are the old entrance to a closed church, where you will sit and wait for the methadone to wash over you and give the relief that your body is craving.

Time Traveller

The bell strikes three. Scrooge is filled with fear: this is the spirit he has feared the most. The Ghost of Christmas Future is here to show Scrooge a future that is yet unwritten. The images he will see are of a future that *could be* if Scrooge follows this path. The time traveller is of the same ilk. He will be joining up the images from the cabbie and the tour guide to give a picture of what could be.

Scrooge is taken to Bob Cratchit's home, and he sees Tiny Tim's crutch hanging on the fireplace. Scrooge realises that Tiny Tim has passed. Scrooge is filled with guilt and regret that he could have done more to save this young soul. This is a sign that Scrooge's walls of denial are starting to crack.

Scrooge is then taken to his home. The servants are in high spirits, they are showing happiness and joy that Scrooge has not witnessed before. He asks the spirit "Why are they so happy?" In that instance, he finds himself in the cemetery and is standing by his grave. They are celebrating his demise.

Scrooge is witnessing his own sad end; he sees that his future is one of a lonely death. Scrooge pleads with the ghost asking if this can be changed. Scrooge's wall of denial is tumbling down and he sees his true self. Scrooge is now seeking his own redemption and is ready to embrace change.

Messenger

The time traveller is the messenger from the future. The time traveller does not speak; he will be taking you through temporal portals. The portals will deliver pictures of a future. A future that could be if you follow your current pathway.

The time traveller can be the bearer of both good and bad news. His purpose is to bring you into consciousness. It is then that you can recognise your Scrooge behaviour. The message from the time traveller will also be prompting change. Will you make an informed decision? A decision that will support a happier, more successful future.

A message has no heart or soul. It's just a format, and its purpose is to say... "Take notice: something needs to be known." This could be an ink-written letter, text or email. The time traveller just delivers the message of what could be. Only you, as the receiver of the message, can decide to respond or ignore.

Fear

Your Scrooge is fear-led. This fear is based on the subconscious mind that has dictated your decision making. The time traveller is now challenging that fear through the images he shows you. The Scrooge behaviour related to fear defined the choices you made yesterday. The tour guide showed you what is. Seeing the truth of what is, enables you to start to connect to the time traveller. When connected, you can hear the message of what could be.

The time traveller is helping you see what your future could look like. What it will look like if Scrooge continues to drive you forward. Scrooge behaviour is fuelled by fear. Fear is the cement that holds denial together. The message will be hard to hear because fear is powerful.

Fear is false evidence appearing real. Fear is driven by the messages you see and hear. You get this within the environments you put yourself within. Marley is the initiator of change. The cabbie and tour guide show you the truth. It is now the turn of the time traveller. He is showing you the future and helping you confront the fear that creates bad decisions.

Denial Breaker

The time traveller is a denial breaker. He is the wrecking ball that swings from the demolition crane. This wrecking ball can smash down the strongest of walls. The time traveller understands the levels of denial that hide your Scrooge behaviour. The time traveller will decide the temporal portal needed. The stronger the message, the larger the wrecking ball.

In the original Dickens' story, the Ghost of Christmas Future's message had to be strong. The denial was huge, and the wrecking ball message needed to have real weight. This was represented in the image of his own grave. Then, Scrooge was taken into the afterlife where his chains were being constructed. The time traveller is also an expert in denial breaking. He knows the messages you need. The time traveller finishes breaking the wall that was loosened by Marley, the cabbie and the tour guide.

The time traveller has been sitting in the background. He has been watching you travel around the mind. He has identified the levels of denial that sit within your Scrooge behaviour. The time traveller will now use this information to deliver the messages. The message that will breach your wall of denial.

Ticking Clock

Tick-tock, tick-tock! This is the sound when you are with the time traveller. It's the subconscious mind telling you that *destiny is coming.* The future is on its way, and nothing will stop it from coming. The ticking clock of time will wait for no one.

The constant ticking and the visions are running through your conscious mind. Are you willing to stay on this path, or is it time to change direction? The ticking clock is a powerful part of the time traveller. The tick-tock makes you aware of your own mortality. You can consider the purpose of the life you have led. The ticking clock represents the time to reflect and review. Review what's been, what is and where you are going...

Crossroads

The time traveller is showing you the shadows of what could be. In the original narrative, Scrooge asks the Ghost of Christmas Future, "Can this be changed?" He asks this question because he sees a crossroads. On one side is the strong vision of what lies ahead. On the other side is a blank canvas of what could be.

The time traveller will say nothing, but stands and points to the path that you are on. This is where your Scrooge behaviour is taking you. At this point, the decision to change is becoming stronger within your mind. The questions of self are coming from the subconscious and into the conscious. These thoughts and questions are starting to create a pathway. This is the pathway towards the blank canvas of a future yet unknown.

Choices

Choices come through thoughts and ideas. The thoughts and ideas have come from the characters that you have met. The time traveller is now showing where your choices will lead. Your decisions are leading you to this point in the future. The true understanding of the choices you have made sit within the inner self. The time traveller's purpose is to confront us with the reality of what will be. Will you continue with the choices and decisions you have been making? Or will you choose a new path?

The sound of the ticking clock and the subconscious screams are getting louder. The screams are becoming clearer. They are also saying, "Change can happen. It does not have to continue this way." The choice is now at the front of your mind... It's decision time.

Decision Time

Scrooge pleaded in front of the Ghost of Christmas Past. Scrooge was ready to make that decision. The time traveller is only the guide to get you to this point.

There will be some Scrooge behaviours that you can easily see. With these, it will be easy to identify the change that is needed. There will be others that have stronger walls of denial that make them harder to see. Denial will lead you to stare into the eyes of the time traveller, stern-faced, arms crossed and saying "I don't believe you." This is denial in full effect.

The time traveller will be delivering you to the place of decision-making. Only you can decide when it's time to change. Only when you choose to change will you hear the singing nightingale.

You make it to the step and lower yourself onto it, slowly. The step is cool, as it is still shaded by the buildings that surround this place. You look up and take in the image before you. There is a busy road crossing with cars bustling to get out and into the next road. The temperature is rising. There is the strong smell of exhaust fumes from the cars that are waiting to move. Across the road, there are small shops, a garage and bars. People are walking up and down the busy street. Some alone; others, together. It's a living world that is passing you by.

You are now just waiting, waiting for the methadone to take effect. You are connected to the conscious mind that keeps saying something needs to change. You can see both the past and present. Both were brought into the conscious by the cabbie and the tour guide.

There is something missing. It is the *what could be if you don't change*. The time traveller is the vehicle that creates thoughts and visions of what could be. The time travel will add images to your mind. These images are linked to the learning from both the cabbie and the tour guide.

The time traveller is now taking you into a future that is filled with fear. As you sit on that step, watching the world go by, you start to think. You think back to the prison years. You take in a breath that is released in a long drawn-out sigh. You can remember all those lonely hours when you lay on that thin prison mattress. You can still feel the criss-crossed metal strips that support the thinnest of mattresses. The pillows that were either as thin as a slice of bread or as hard as a concrete block. All you ever had for company was your thoughts.

Eight years of your life were wasted behind those thick, bleak walls. Walls that offered you nothing but the knowledge that you were trapped and going nowhere. You suddenly have a realisation. In truth, you are just moving towards another prison sentence.

Last year, you were sat in Winchester Prison. It's a place you know well. You can see yourself leaning against the wall looking out at the wing. Winchester is an old Victorian jail that has three landings with all the cells around the edge. In between the landings is a mesh that is there to stop people jumping off or pushing someone else over. As you stand there, you can feel the tension that sits in the air. Violence is always present. Everyone is on guard and pre-empting what could or may happen next.

You can smell the pine disinfectant. The smell is not quite overriding the smell of the urine from the urinals. You look at a young group of prisoners playing pool. There is a haze of smoke as they puff away on their matchstick-thin roll-ups. 90% of the population smokes, and they will smoke whatever is available. What wouldn't you give to be standing in a summer meadow, smelling the freshness of a thriving life? The smell here is as lifeless as the walls that keep you locked in.

"How's you, Gethin?" it's the voice of Mr B, you have known Mr B since you were fifteen years old. You reply saying "I'm OK, just waiting for bang-up." Mr B then says, "Gethin, I have watched you grow up from a boy to man. If you don't change, you will go from being the youngest person in this prison to the oldest." He then walks off towards the group of younger lads that are playing pool.

His words are ringing in your ears. You look towards the end of the wing and notice a swooper (this is someone who walks the wings, picking up old cigarette butts). He is frail and looks to be in his late 80s. In truth, he is not yet 70. The system has aged him. He is completely alone. No friends or family visit him. He was left alone many years ago.

The time traveller is beckoning you towards him. As he enters your consciousness, you start to think about the many friends that you have lost through suicide, overdose and mental illness. You feel another tear as you think of your dear friend Mike. Mike hung himself in Winchester Prison when he was just nineteen years of age. You loved Mike as a brother. You grew up in care together and then graduated into the prison system.

Mike was a physically strong young man, and he always presented as mentally strong. You knew Mike's story. It was one full of immeasurable pain. Although you were not there on that fateful night, you know what was in his mind. Mike would have sat in that cold, heartless cell looking at what had been, where he was now and the future that awaited him. Mike would only have seen more pain and a darkness that filled every part of who he was. It was this pain that led to the decision to take his young life.

Tears are streaming down your face, and you're sobbing into your hands. The pain of losing your best friend is causing you to shake. The quiet sobbing is now a cry that is filled with loneliness and loss. Your heart is a heavy weight that is causing you to sink deeper and deeper into despair.

You have a recurring thought. Is this my future? Will I one day make this decision? Will suicide be the doorway to my eventual end? Will I be another one of those addicts who die in a doorway with a needle still resting in their hand? The time traveller is showing you a future that is smashing through the denial. It's the message of your true existence and eventual end.

You hear a shout, and you're jolted back into the now. It's a car driver who is shouting at someone who cut him up. You start to consider what the cabbie, the tour guide and time traveller have shown you. You have seen your destiny and the future is in your hands. It's now up to you to decide if your life is going to be a success or a failure? In *A Christmas Carol*, Scrooge connected with this future. He saw that he was destined to a lonely death and, at that point, he made a decision to change.

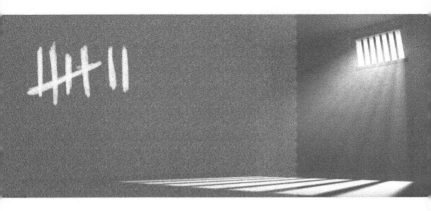

Singing Nightingale

Singing nightingales are all around you. They are the ones that offer you support and guidance. Scrooge behaviour prevents you from hearing the song they sing.

In Dickens' tale, Scrooge's nephew Fred visited him late-afternoon on Christmas Eve. He offered his uncle Scrooge a place at his table on Christmas Day. Scrooge refused with a *Bah! Humbug!* Unfortunately, Scrooge was so trapped in his world of greed and mistrust that he was unable to accept the offer. This would never deter his nephew, Fred. He would never give up on his uncle, Scrooge. No. Nephew Fred would keep singing his song.

The next time Scrooge saw his nephew was when he was with the Ghost of Christmas Present. At that moment, he witnessed his nephew defending him. That was when Scrooge started hearing the song being sung by his singing nightingale. Scrooge's mind was starting to open.

By Christmas Day, Scrooge had broken down his wall of denial. Scrooge knew that the chance of redemption was within his reach. Scrooge put on his hat, scarf and coat and made his way to nephew Fred's home. On entering the home, Scrooge asked if there was still a place for him at the table. His nephew Fred held no judgement and welcomed Scrooge with open arms.

Unconditional Love

Think about a time when you were unwell, hurt or lost. At all these times, singing nightingales appeared; they loved you unconditionally. When Scrooge is in control, you will be blinded and won't see them. Scrooge had his nephew Fred, he was Scrooge's singing nightingale. Fred was always there unconditionally loving his cantankerous Uncle Scrooge. Unfortunately, dear Scrooge was so caught up in himself that he could not hear him.

Generous

The characters of the mind have torn down the wall of denial. The Scrooge pattern of behaviour has been exposed. Exposing the Scrooge behaviour released the grip it has had on your life. Once released the sun comes out, the light fills the here and now. At this point, you can hear the singing nightingales.

The singing nightingales smile with love and generosity. They want to help you. They just want you to experience happiness. This happiness sits within the human soul. At that point, the Scrooge behaviour is cracking. It's like dried mud that sticks to the legs of children who mudlark on the Thames.

The singing nightingales hold out their hands. They offer a generosity that exists without any charge. Singing nightingales are like our friend Marley. His selfless, altruistic ways have led us to this point. The singing nightingales are the next stage. They will guide you to a new way of being. Your singing nightingale could be a friend, family member, colleague or even a complete stranger.

Compassion/Empathy

Compassion for others is a what separates us from other species. We want to help the old, the disabled and the troubled. Other species will abandon them to protect the long-term survival of the species. The singing nightingales in your world feel compassion for you. This compassion will drive them to want to help you succeed. When this compassion connects with your heart, you will start to grow.

Singing nightingales have an abundance of empathy and compassion. When you look back, you can see the changes that empathy and compassion can bring. In the 1800s it was the affluent who brought about change. Their empathy and compassion led to the demolition of the slums and opened the door to human rights and equality for all. The empathy and compassion of your singing nightingales can help you move away from the slums of your mind. The slums are where Scrooge dominates.

Singing nightingales empathise with your pain. This drives the compassion and the desire to help you. They see the need for change way before you become aware of it. Denial and close-mindedness prevented you from hearing the singing nightingales. Now that the wall is down, you can hear their sweet song that can support change.

Hope/Belief

Singing nightingales are waiting for you. They are filled with a limitless supply of hope. This is not false hope. Singing nightingales have many examples of seeing people change.

Everyone has the capacity to change. This is your moment. Marley, the cabbie, the tour guide and the time traveller broke down the wall of denial. Your mind is now open. Scrooge has been pulled out of the shadows so you can see the truth.

The previous characters live and work within your mind. The difference with the singing nightingales is that they live in the real world. The characters in the mind guide you into their waiting hands. Singing nightingales have a hope that runs eternal. They are waiting to separate you from Scrooge. They will bring you back into the world of personal and professional success.

Negative beliefs enabled you to hold on to Scrooge. Those behaviours led you to this day. These beliefs were broken down by Marley, the cabbie, the tour guide and the time traveller. The singing nightingales now take over. They have absolute belief in who you are. They see your true self. The singing nightingales believe in you until you start to believe in yourself.

Faith

You too are also a singing nightingale. This part of you lives on the pathway between the head and the heart. The heart pumps the blood around the body. In the same way, the heart fills the singing nightingale with faith. This faith is pumped to the mind. Faith and belief in yourself will grow. After growing your faith, you share it with those around you.

Faith and belief are the lifeblood of change. Faith and belief that come from the heart are flooding the slums of the mind. Those same slums that have held you back. The momentum of faith and belief will carry you. You have gone from the closed mindset to the growth mindset.

Joining your faith with the faith of the singing nightingales is key. The joining of these faiths is the way to break away from Scrooge. Scrooge entrapped you in the squalor of the mind. Redemption is before you. It's now time to escape the Whitechapel slums of the mind.

Honesty

Honesty is the cornerstone of the singing nightingale. This cornerstone is as strong as the cornerstone that holds up St

Paul's. The singing nightingale's honesty will be instrumental in any change. The singing nightingale will become your vital, critical friend.

The singing nightingale will not collude with any Scrooge behaviour. They will be honest. They will offer suggestions and thoughts on the path being travelled. If the singing nightingale moved away from the truth, they would become a fellow Scrooge. Your Scrooges will be engrossed in conversation and stories. Suddenly you will both look up and see you have left the light of the path. You would again be lost within a forest of shadows. Watch out for complacency.

You lift your head and wipe the tears from your cheeks. The methadone has kicked in. The aching of the muscles has disappeared, and the sweats have gone too. You take off your jacket as you start to feel the comfortable warmth of the sun.

It's time to go, but where? You look left and right, but neither has any relevance. They both lead to the same place, nowhere. You turn right and start to walk. Your head hangs low, staring at the grubby, stained pathing slabs. You are now looking for cigarette butts as you have not had a fag in an hour. This is yet another obsession that starts to take control of your mind.

You are not aware yet, but something has happened inside your mind. The characters within your mind have torn down your wall of denial. For the first time in over twenty years, you are going to feel something. Singing nightingales have been all around you. They were prison officers, probation officers, support workers and family. Your Scrooge's denial meant you could not hear the songs they sang.

Suddenly you hear a voice, "Gethin, you OK?" You look up into the smiling face of Jo. Little do you realise but at that moment you have found your singing nightingale. Jo is a support worker who has been involved in your life for the last three years. Jo has offered you nothing but support and care. Jo has tried to lead you to a better way of living. The Scrooge within ignored this offer of support. Scrooge would never accept the help being offered.

You look at Jo and simply say, "Yes, I'm OK." At that moment, Jo sees into your eyes. Jo connects with all the pain and despair that has been your life; the wasted life of the last twenty years. Little do you realise that at that one moment you are connected to her. The wall of denial is breached. Jo says one sentence to you. This seemingly meaningless sentence is the catalyst that brings on a complete transformation. The transformation from who you once were to who you are now.

"Gethin," she says, "you need to book yourself in somewhere." You know what she means; you need to go into a drug-treatment centre. It was nothing that you hadn't heard before. But wait, something was different... You are feeling something. What is going on?

You feel a smile move to your lips. You feel an inner warmth that starts to wrap around your heart. Suddenly the cold rock that sits heavy in your chest explodes. You feel your heart burst into life. It starts to pound, and the blood is now rushing around your once lifeless body.

You believed what Jo said. For the first time in your life, you both heard and felt the words. You could hear the singing nightingale. You say to Jo, "Yes, you are right and I will book in to see my key worker." Something else was different. You believed what you had just said, and knew that you would follow the words with action.

That's it, its *Action.* That's what you needed, that is how you would change. Your singing nightingales would show you what needed to be done. But if you truly wanted change, it was you that would need to put in the action. You thank Jo and walk away with a smile on your face and hope in your heart. At that point, neither of you knew what had taken place. There was no way you could ever imagine what was to come.

As you start walking home, you start to really notice your surroundings. They all seem different. Why is that? You have walked this path so many times before. It's because this time the mind is clear and you can see what has always been there.

You stop outside the bike shop. The sun is shining brightly against the windows. Your brow scrunches as the eyes squint. You move to the window and lift your hand to shade the eyes. There are many bikes in there. Mountain bikes, racers, men's, women's, children's. It's a rainbow of colour, red, green, pink, blue. You feel that smile again as you have a thought that says, "One day you can go in here and buy a bike." This is an honest thought, and you believe in this thought. You know, with action, the bike will be yours. You turn and walk back home. This time you are not looking at the floor, you're looking at the horizon in front of you.

The Hobblers

There are always people around that need your support. When you are trapped by Scrooge, you will not see them because you are wrapped up in yourself. Charles Dickens' Scrooge saw Bob Cratchit every day. Bob Cratchit was a hobbler and never once did Scrooge see that he could help. Why? Because Scrooge was obsessed by his greed.

On that Christmas Eve, Scrooge begrudgingly let Bob have Christmas Day off. Scrooge showed no gratitude or interest in Bob, he just told him to be in extra early on Boxing Day. On that fateful night, Scrooge visited Bob's home with the Ghost of Christmas Present. It was at that moment Scrooge witnessed the poverty in which Bob and his family were living.

Scrooge also came face to face with Tiny Tim. Tiny Tim was an innocent soul who was suffering from ill health. Scrooge was starting to see the reality of today and the impact his greed had on those around him.

Scrooge's real moment of truth came when he again visited the home with the Ghost of Christmas Future. On that second visit, he could see the sadness in the home as Bob and his wife mourned the passing of Tiny Tim.

Scrooge decided on that Christmas morning that he was going to help, and he started by sending a prize turkey to the Cratchit's home. But Scrooge did not end there. On Boxing Day, he raised Bob's salary and promised to support Tiny Tim's treatment. Scrooge finally realised that true happiness came from giving. Greed had only fed him misery.

Giving Back

There were two pivotal moments in *A Christmas Carol*. The first was when Scrooge witnessed the plight of Tiny Tim. At that moment, Scrooge connected with his reality. The next pivotal moment was in the future when Scrooge saw Tiny Tim's crutch resting against the fireplace. Scrooge experienced empathy and sadness for the pain of Tim's family.

On the day of Scrooge's redemption, he saw that he could help Tim. He knew he had the gift that could change the destiny of this innocent soul. There are many souls in the world that need help. I call these *the hobblers,* and you're their singing nightingale. You now have the gift to guide them along the path to happiness.

Giving back is also the gift we give to ourselves. This will only happen when we give back selflessly. The world we live in today is filled with greed (Scrooge). There are lots of opinions that say, "We should not give anything for free." Bah! Humbug! to this. Giving back is the gift that keeps on giving.

Humility

Humility is the key component when supporting hobblers. The message needs to come from humility and not from the ego. Ego is Scrooge, and you dissolve it by giving unconditionally.

When you start telling others about the great things you do, you are not giving freely. You are giving for a reward. You are looking for the praise of others and their acknowledgement. Self-seeking feeds your ego, the voice telling you that you are great and good. The ego is not attractive to hobblers on the pathway. The ego is the doorway back to Scrooge. When you engage with ego, you are on the way back to Newgate Prison.

On the other hand, humility is attractive. The hobblers are naturally attracted to humility. They want to connect with your singing nightingale. They will take your hand so you can lead them into the light. This is a future that is filled with unlimited opportunities.

Purpose

The principle that underpins the masterful change is giving back. It's this giving back that gives purpose to life. The purpose is both for you and them. Giving them the gift that helped you will give them freedom. They will then have the ability to give the gift to others.

Life needs to have purpose. What is your purpose? Is it to gain wealth and status? A place in history? Something else that sits outside of you? Could your new purpose be about giving back? There are many hobblers, and they need your guidance.

Values

Life-giving values are something that Scrooge never showed to the world. Marley can see the true values that sit within your heart. It was the cabbie, the tour guide and the time traveller that opened your heart and mind. They enabled the singing nightingale to be heard.

Whilst delivering the gift you will connect with your true values. The values that make you truly human. Loyalty, self-respect, kindness, true justice and honesty, to name but a few. These values are what supports the process of masterful change. Your values are seen and admired by those around you.

These values enable the hobblers to connect. The hobblers will connect with your singing nightingale's values. They will not just *see* your selflessness; they will *feel* it. They will know that you just want to help. When you use your values, they grow and multiply. More will start to appear within your conscious self. These values have always sat within you but were hidden by Scrooge. This process has opened the chest of awareness. You have revealed the true self and unlocked a treasure trove of values within.

Self-Love

Self-love comes from delivering the gift to hobblers. When you love others, you love yourself. When you love yourself, you will attract love back. You no longer need to have Scrooge's greed. Greed is the cloud within the mind that blocks the sunlight of self-love.

Love is a pin on the edge of the key retrieved by Marley. He brought this up from the unconscious mind. Learning to love and give self-love comes with the understanding and accepting of who you are. To love yourself is to accept yourself unconditionally.

It is only when you love yourself unconditionally that you can then offer true love to others. This is the essence of masterful change within you. You need to remember that not everyone is able to connect with the love you offer. This does not mean they are at fault; they are just not ready. On these occasions, we need to step back and leave them in the hands of Marley. All you need do is let them know the gift can be delivered when they are ready.

Human

Being human is a concept that can be lost within the lives we live. I was once told, "We are human beings, not human doings." The mind is always saying, "this will make us truly happy, try this or that." We are all so busy doing and chasing the next thing within our lives. Whilst chasing, we forget what it's like to just be. We miss the experience of now. We disconnect from being truly human.

True happiness sits within you. It's not outside of you. Masterful change is the deliverer of this great gift. When delivering the gift, you are being human. Connecting in the moment of now with another human being is a true gift. Not wanting, not doing, just being is what makes us truly human.

Forgiveness

Forgiving yourself is the main purpose of the masterful change. Forgiveness starts with the forgiving of yourself. When you give the gift to the hobblers, you are being kind to yourself. Being kind to yourself is the road to forgiving and accepting who you once were. Once you forgive and accept, you will start to understand and love who you are now.

You can never go back and undo what was done. What you must do is forgive yourself and those that may have harmed you. Forgiveness allows us to see that we are all human. You can now stop beating yourself up and judging those around you.

The forgiveness process is a long road. There are many paths that lead off the road of true redemption. At times, they will look attractive. You may say, "I'm not forgiving that," or "I'm not forgiving this," and "I can't forgive myself." Having the singing nightingales by your side keeps you on the path of forgiveness.

The centre arm of the key that was retrieved by Marley is forgiveness. Marley will sometimes ask you to deliver this gift to those you see as undeserving. It may be hobblers who may have harmed or hurt you. He asks you to do this as he knows the true meaning of forgiveness. Forgiving those who have hurt you, is a very powerful thing. Doing this is living the masterful change. Masterful change sits within our actions.

Inner Peace

Inner peace is contentment with self. Contentment comes from being comfortable with the decisions and choices that you make today. You create your own inner peace. This is done through commitment, knowledge and understanding. They all sit within the positive choices you are making today.

All the elements that make up your mind, body and soul are working in unison. Marley, the cabbie, the tour guide, the time traveller and your singing nightingales are here. They are supporting you to be the very best you can be.

With this inner peace, you are within masterful change. You will be coming from a place of true value and humility. It is now that you will see the hobblers and offer them the gift of support. Passing on this gift will give you more inner peace. You will get this by guiding them on the pathway to their own inner peace.

You make it back to the flat and walk through the door. You are struck by the smell of rotten rubbish from the bin bag that has been sitting there for days. The smell is overpowering. It is mid-afternoon and the sun that has been burning through the closed windows. The heat has turned the flat into an oven.

You go into every room and open the windows. You then sit in the chair that has swallowed all your dreams for many years. You sit there, considering your plan of getting yourself into detox. You then think, "But what then?" You're thirty-five and have no qualifications, no work history and no real understanding of what you could do.

Your mind starts to wander. You think of all those singing nightingales that have tried to help you. Maybe that is your purpose, maybe you can help people. Yes, that's what you can do, but first you need to help yourself. You suddenly become aware of the mess that you're sitting in. The next thought is one that shocks you. "Let's clean this place up." You smile and realise that this is the first step to taking care of yourself.

You walk into the bedroom. You step over the clothes and rubbish that covers the floor. You see an old carrier bag by the window that you can use for rubbish. As you take the bag, you look out of the window and see an old friend of yours, Nick. Nick is an addict and has been sleeping on the street for years. He is hobbling along on his crutch. You know he is going off to score another dose of heroin. Your heart goes out to him. You know that he is the person you want to help in the future. He has nothing and no one in his life. Nick's hope disappeared many years ago.

You turn from the window and start to pick up the rubbish that is on the floor. You throw the stained clothes that haven't been washed for months onto the bed. Cleaning yourself up is going to be harder than cleaning up this flat. If you want to create a masterful change, you need to persevere.

You stand in the doorway of the bedroom and it is a different room, the cool-fresh air is coming through the window. The dirty clothes are in a corner ready to be washed. You have put a duvet on the bed. It now looks like a welcoming space. Not just a place to hide away from the world around you. The floor is now clear, and you stand there, feeling proud. A warm glow comes over you and a deep inner sense that it will be OK.

You then make your way to the kitchen. Your eyes take in the view. You can see the used needles that are scattered on the worktop. You see the blunt needle that you pushed into your neck this morning. You shudder as you remember the life you woke up to, just this morning. You know you are soon to leave it, but right now this is your reality. You acknowledge it but want to hide it from sight. As you start to clear the needles, you start to remember some of the other memories. The memories that you saw through the Cabbie's window.

You remember the children's homes. The detention centre. The children's secure unit and the eleven prisons you have been to. You remember the partners you have lost. The daughter that was adopted. You stop what you're doing and lean against the kitchen window. You feel the warm, wet tears of regret that are falling down your cheeks to your lips. You taste the familiar saltiness of the many tears you have shed for these memories.

You suddenly hear a child laughing and look down into the garden. You wipe away the tears. The laughter is not the same as you heard from the playground, that was just a sound. A sound that had no depth or feeling. This laughter is different as you are now connected to the world. You can hear the joy that the child is sharing. You can also sense the happiness that the child is feeling. You get another feeling of inner peace. The internal thought of "It's going to be OK," is getting stronger. The inner peace is being delivered from the heart to the mind. It is that feeling of peace that says, "Everything is just as it is meant to be."

You turn back to the kitchen. You start to gather up the many dirty syringes that are laying on the sides and floor. Every-one represents the self-loathing and harm that you delivered into your veins. You collect them all up and place them in the bag.

You then start to wipe the stains from the sides. Dried food, tea stains and numerous spots of blood. How could you live in a place like this? You then empty the sink of the stale, discoloured water. It smells like the Thames at low tide. The tideline is thick with scum. You know you will soon be washing away the scum that sits within your mind. The kitchen now looks like a place for cooking food. It's no longer a place to cook your daily doses of heroin. You are now seeing that these small choices and actions are having a positive impact.

You make it into the front room. As you take in the sight, you realise that to create masterful change you will need to change everything. Every room is now ready for the world to see except this one. This room is like your mind, it is in chaos. You know that to clear your mind will take dedication and action. This is your first step, and you make the decision to get this done too.

You can hardly see the floor for the rubbish. There are also broken butts, and there is ash everywhere. You start picking up the rubbish, placing it into the bag you found in the kitchen. The rubbish is soon thrown into the bag, but the room is still in a terrible state. You have no Hoover and must get on your hands and knees with a dustpan and brush. As you kneel, you can feel the solid concrete floor. The hard floor is felt below the wafer-thin carpet on your knees. You wince as your knees are weak and have little fat to cushion them. This is the consequence of a mind that chooses heroin over food.

Whilst on your knees, the smell of the butts and ash is stronger than ever. It is mixed with the stench of the rotten rubbish that has sat there for months. The smell is the same as you get when you enter the bin sheds downstairs. You push yourself on, and before you know it, the carpet is clear.

The only two things in the room are an old big box TV and armchair. The TV was your only company on those long lonely nights. The armchair had no comfort but was far better than the floor. You wipe the dust, tea stains and black ash from the top of the TV. There is a thick layer of grime on the screen. This must have affected you seeing the clear images on the TV. Cleaning this screen represents the clearing of the mind. Once the mind is cleared, you will then see a true vision of the future.

You finally turn to the chair. It is such a sorry sight! The arms have thick black stains, and the cushion is split, showing the foam inside. You scrub the arms with a damp cloth from the kitchen. You then puff up the cushions. They have been squashed with an imprint of the body that has sat lifeless for so long.

It is done, the whole flat is now a liveable space. You can now see how in the future you can make this into a home. It will be a place that you can feel safe and comfortable in and be proud of. You have hope, faith and belief. This hope, faith and belief are fuelling your inner peace.

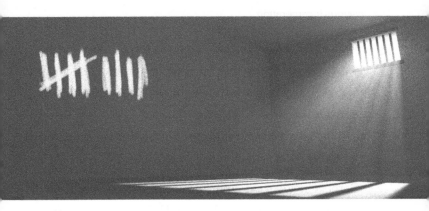

Masterful Change

Masterful change is a transformation that happens within. It's not what we show the world, but what we believe within. Ebenezer Scrooge had been on a journey of self-discovery. What was, what is and what could be.

This experience led him to see that true salvation had to come from within. This is true for you too. If you want your world to be different, then *you* need to change. When you change, the world will change with you. This is related to natural laws that have no rhyme or reason. *Good attracts good* and *bad attracts bad*.

How do we know that Scrooge had this internal shift? We saw it on that Christmas morning. Ebenezer woke with joy in his heart and a desire to make things right. Ebenezer threw open the window. It was a clear, crisp winter's day, with snow on the ground. Ebenezer saw a boy and asked, "What day is it?" The boy replied, "Why, it's Christmas Day."

At this point, Ebenezer knew that redemption was before him. This was his moment to make things right with himself and the world around him. Ebenezer's change was immediate, he started doing things that he would never have done before. He paid the boy to get a turkey for the Cratchit's. He paid a cab driver to deliver it. Scrooge chuckled as he knew this was something he would not have done the day before. The external act of giving reflects the internal desire to help.

Scrooge made good on his promise. To Tiny Tim, who did not die, he became a second father. He became a good friend, a good master and as good a man as was possible. Ebenezer's masterful change meant that he became someone who brought joy to both himself and others.

Freedom

Waking on that final morning, Scrooge was unaware of the chains. The chains that had weighed heavy on his life. Scrooge had been visited by four spirits. These spirits opened his eyes to the world around him. You are now aware of your four characters within your mind. Marley, the cabbie, the tour guide and the time traveller. They are the vehicle that will lead *you* towards true freedom.

Marley is your instigator of change. Marley stands at the doorway of your freedom. He is helping you recognise who you are and where you are going. Marley understands the journey that needs to be travelled. The journey that will lead you to freedom.

True freedom is being present within the now. In the now, you can recognise the past decisions that led you here today. Freedom starts with understanding yourself. This understanding and the actions which follow are where change comes from. Awareness is in the now. Using this awareness creates meaningful change. Meaningful change is freedom from making the same mistakes over and over again.

The freedom that comes from change is a visual clearing of your storm clouds. The skies will clear, the sun will shine through. You will start seeing all that was once missed. Quieting the behaviours of Scrooge allows you to smell the scent of the coffee, the freshness of the bread that seeps out of the bakery next door.

Experiencing

Once you cross the threshold from subconscious to conscious, you enter the light of the living. Being conscious means you are experiencing the now. In the now you can connect to yourself and those around you. Amazing things happen every minute of every day. Becoming conscious will help you live a life that is full of experience.

Masterful change allows this to happen. Today you are freed from the slums of your mind. You don't just see the world, you experience it. During a sunset, there is more than just the beauty of the visual experience. There is also the deeper warm feeling that rises within. This is sparked by the colours that dance across the sky. When truly connected, a smile reaches your lips. At this point, you do not just see the sunset, you are truly present. You are part of the beauty that lays before you.

The experience of life is a beautiful thing. It is the tapestry that has been delicately woven by both you and those around you. As with any tapestry, you need to understand the meaning, understand the story it is telling you. My friend, this is your story and it sits within your experiences.

Love

I have already mentioned cornerstones. Love is not just the cornerstone; it is the cement that runs through your masterful change. Love is not for others, it's for you. The wanting and needing to take care and love yourself unconditionally.

Your decisions dictate if you give yourself love or pain. Scrooge is the giver of pain. Remember, he is forever present within you, he is going nowhere. Self-love and awareness are what keeps him at bay. Whenever a decision needs to be made, ask this question, "Will this change be loving to me?"

Once you love yourself, you can pass this onto others. You will witness the Scrooge behaviours in others. You will witness the pain they give themselves. Your connection with empathy means you can offer them your love. The love you will be offering them is the passing of this gift. The gift that change is possible for them too.

Understanding

Understanding your Scrooge behaviours brings new meaning into your life. Changing Scrooge behaviour means that your life now has a real purpose. On Christmas Day, Scrooge awoke with that feeling of redemption. He realised that it was not too late to change.

You now have the understanding that you can create a new you. You are starting the journey of loving and accepting yourself. You can embrace new ideas make new decisions and create the person you truly want to be. Ebenezer also knew that there was work to be done. He understood the importance of maintaining his masterful change. Scrooge understood he needed to maintain awareness. This awareness would avoid him slipping down the path once travelled.

Understanding reminds you how to maintain continuous freedom. Your freedom will depend on continuous action in the now. Complacency is within the shadows of the mind. You need to stay vigilant so as not to walk blindly back to the mind's version of Newgate Prison. Freedom sits within you. Your freedom depends on how you live your today. Always remember and understand that the subconscious mind is still very much at work. You will find yourself drifting down that road. Today your understanding is within the conscious mind. You are no longer led by your Scrooge behaviour.

The life you are experiencing today is a gift, and this is a gift that needs to be treasured. Every day, this gift can give you something new, but like any gift it needs to be delicately unwrapped. Once unwrapped, you will be able to see the beauty that lies within the beautiful package of today. Today you understand how the gift is both unwrapped and given to those hobblers who need it.

Blank Canvas

Your life is a blank canvas. It's now time to paint a world that is filled with beauty and colour. Your Scrooge is no longer in control and anything is possible. You are now the artist who can visualise the life you want. It is a life full of endless opportunities.

What an amazing picture you can paint! Your palette is freedom, experiences, love. Your brushes are the understanding and wisdom that has been gifted to you. These gifts have been delivered by the characters within your mind. The blank canvas represents the endless opportunities that sit before you.

It's time to start painting a new future without Scrooge. He is no longer a part of this future. Your future is now dictated by new behaviours. These behaviours create new decisions and choices.

Wisdom

Your wisdom throws light onto your Scrooge. You now know what your Scrooge really looks like. The wisdom within will drive your change. This wisdom knows what to do to move you forward. You are moving into a bright new world that sits before you. The wisdom and understanding of yourself will take away the dark clouds. You are now walking into the clear blue skies of a summer day.

The wisdom that sits within you today is more valuable than any precious stone. This wisdom will lead to peace of the heart.

You now have the understanding and wisdom of what fed your Scrooge. Today you are saying, "Scrooge no more."

Beacon of Hope

You are believing and changing. You are ready to become the beacon of hope. You are the future that is not yet written. The understanding of what was, what is, and what could be is a gift. This gift gives you a new way to make decisions and choices.

You are the street artist that sets up his pastels in the public square. As artists do, you start to sketch, with the hobblers watching and wondering what you are creating. As the artist, you have a vision within your mind and you are transferring this vision onto the pavement for all to see.

You are now the masterful change. You are the beacon of hope. The hobblers on the path are observing the changes that moved you away from Scrooge. They are impressed by what you are sketching. They are holding out their hands to masterful change. They can hear the singing nightingale that's within you.

Masterful change is like the pebble that ripples out on the pond. You are that pebble. When you change the ripples flow out. The belief in yourself is seen by all of those around you. Your ripples will connect with those you meet on the pathway to your personal freedom.

The intervention of Marley, meeting the cabbie, the tour guide and time traveller have opened your eyes to a reality of endless opportunities. They have enabled the singing nightingales to open the floodgates to your heart. It's now time to unleash the power of love and belief in yourself. You now have the ability to change anything... You can, you will, you shall...

Today is an immeasurable distance from the person you once were. Every day you wake up, and a smile hits your face. You realise that you are free from the prison of your mind. The prison that entrapped you into a way of thinking. This thinking stunted and separated you from all of those who entered your life.

On that final day, you woke up completely trapped by Scrooge. You were lost, lonely, scared and fearful. You were disconnected from everything and everyone. You were the living dead. You were just a criminal junkie that had given up on life.

Today, you do not dismiss the pain and suffering that you endured. You embrace it. The first thirty-five years of your life made you the person you are today. The characters within your mind have shown you the truth of your experiences. You now see how you can use these experiences to take care of your today. You now use this to become the singing nightingale. You are the singing nightingale for the hobblers that you meet every day.

At this moment, right here, right now, you have knowledge. You can see how your experiences in life led you to this point. It is said that *wisdom comes from experience, not age*. A wise man or woman will use their own experiences and those of others to shape their today. Imagine a 50-year-old beggar sitting on the dirty streets of London's Whitechapel. He has sat in that same spot for years and years. Every day he sits, cap in hand. If you asked him for some wise words, he would reply, "After 10 pm you will be less likely to get your shilling for a bed in the doss house." Why? Because this is his only experience.

Sometimes you look back at yourself sitting in that chair. When you do, it feels like you're looking back at someone else. Your transformation has been as dramatic as was our dear old friend Scrooge's. You realise now that Marley and the other characters within this story helped you connect. You connected to a pool of wisdom that was always within you. You connected to your resilience and ability to survive.

Wisdom is the fuel for your change. The cabbie in your mind connected the memories that gave you understanding. Understanding and learning developed into the wisdom that supported your decision-making.

When you began searching for a purpose. You remembered seeing Nick out of the bedroom window. He was another lost drug addict walking the path you had been travelling. This laid the foundation for your new future. A future that practises giving back with humility and not ego.

At the end of that final day, you were lying in bed. Physically, nothing had changed. You were still dependent on heroin. What had changed was your whole mindset. As you lay there, you felt the warm, comforting peace that had entered you. You were thinking about all the possibilities that lay before you. You had the belief that positive change was coming. You had connected to an inner strength that would support you in the years ahead. This feeling has stayed with you ever since.

Lying in that bed was like lying on a warm meditation beach. The rising tide was the tiredness that was washing over you. The warm, soft sand that cushioned your body was the bed that lay below you. The warmth from the sun was the duvet that tucked you in.

For the first time in years, you turn and snuggle into the pillow. You slowly fall into the most peaceful sleep. At this moment, you are safe in the knowledge that all is going to be OK.

Marley, the cabbie, the tour guide, the time traveller and your singing nightingales are with you. The loneliness disappears as does the day. It truly is the beginning of the end.

Conclusion

During this journey, you will have identified your Scrooge behaviours. The behaviours and parts of you that have had a negative effect on your life. You have these behaviours like everyone else does. When do you know they have been active? When you say, "Why does this always happen to me?" The truthful answer is, *it is you.* Yes, *you* who made it happen. Your Scrooge was taking control of your life.

Marley has always been swimming around in your mind. You can sense him in that uncomfortable feeling in your belly. The needle thought in your mind. Fear of change is what held you back, and that is why you need the other characters.

Whilst with the cabbie you collected the memories of what once was. The cabbie gave you the opportunity to start seeing your Scrooge. Procrastination, arrogance, close-mindedness, unwillingness, self-indulgence, to name but a few. These behaviours sit within the memories that the cabbie showed you.

With the decisions and memories of yesterday, you became ready for the tour guide. The tour guide gave you the truth of your today. Having been with the cabbie you now have the experience of your past. This is where the wall of denial starts to come down. You see the patterns of behaviour that have blocked your growth.

At this point, the tour guide is introduced. The tour guide has shown you the reality of your today. During the time with the tour guide, self-honesty was the key. Self-honesty shines the light and exposes Scrooge. The tour guide asks the questions of your today. Is this what you want? Are you happy with your lot? The answers to these questions will show you your today. With this understanding, the tour guide will give you the next question. "What could you change?"

You were brave enough to go with the time traveller. The time traveller smashed down the last of the denial. It is only after the denial is gone that you can see where you are going. You now have the evidence of who your Scrooge is. You now have the understanding of today. You see the impact Scrooge is having. This is the time to transform learning into wisdom. That is the truth of the time traveller. Honestly looking at what was, what is and recognising what will be.

The denial is gone. Your Scrooge is lit up by the light of the lamp. Now the only thing that will support change is *action*. The action comes from the support of your singing nightingales. They are all around you. It's time to listen and hear what they say. In life, we all need the support of others to develop and grow. It takes courage to hear what is being said. It will take even more courage to accept it. Once you accept it, you will be empowered to change. Change will only ever come from continuous action.

Masterful change is an amazing achievement. Connecting with it will bring pride in who you are. Masterful change will be witnessed by those within your life. They will be amazed at the changes in who you are now. Your masterful change will inspire them to change as well.

With the insight of this development programme you now have the ability to see other people's Scrooge behaviours. These others are the hobblers. At this point, the magic of the programme is revealed. Now you are able to share the gift of what you have learnt. Freely giving this gift will give you as much as it gives them.

"*You keep what you have by giving it away.*" This is true of this development programme. The selfless act of giving will feed the values and principles that disempower the Scrooge within.

Now it is *your* time to go out there and be free. Free from the chains that have held you back. Go live a life that is full of value. Today is the first day of the story that is not yet written.

There is another magical gift that will come from this development programme. It is how you will be giving to those who truly need it. A percentage of the payment for the services you buy will help do something amazing: I am going to offer this development programme to services and charities that support the most vulnerable in society.

You will be giving back the gift that can change lives. Lives like mine. Charities and services brought me back from the gates of hell. You will now have the opportunity to support services like these. You will save lives. My friend, you will give them a gift that is far greater than you could ever imagine. The gift of living a life that is full of opportunity.

Acknowledgements

Many people have been part of my journey both personally and therapeutically. Without the support and inspiration of the following people this book would not be in your hands now. Thank you.

Alan Rhoddan was the first counsellor I felt connected with the true Gethin Jones and could share my past decisions with. Allan opened the door to the life I have today.

John McCarthy is a psychotherapist with a deep wisdom and a therapeutic understanding of both thought and behaviour. He has also been a huge influence when setting up *Unlocking Potential*, sharing the evidence base that sits within the programmes I deliver.

The many Singing Nightingales that supported my development–Jo Purdy, Debbie Willis, Joanne Ross, Bonnie Brooks, Tony Weeks, Stuart McDowell, Cecile Todd, Bruce Marr, Chris Carter, Paul Baker, Ian Walker, Hillary Stainton, Rhona Walker.

Finally, I need to say a special thank you to my family. Though we went through difficult times we all found a way to love in our own unique way...

Mum, Adele Hodge, Paige Hodge, Jordan Hodge, Miriam Jones, Brandon Sawyer, Megan Sawyer, Sadie Jones, Lacey Jones, Louise Jones, Sean Jones, Alfie Jones, Karen Gibbs, Tilly Stewart, Henry Stewart and my little Ellie x

About Gethin

Gethin is not your typical behaviour change specialist with an academic pedigree. He is an effective behaviour change specialist for others because he has engineered dramatic changes in his own behaviour.

Gethin has been there, done that (usually getting caught in the process!) and gone back again.

Gethin grew up in care, spent eight years in prison, was an intravenous drug user for many years and was on a clear path of repeated prison sentences and an eventual early death.

His own transformation finally began in 2000 when he embarked on a six-year therapeutic journey incorporating psychotherapy, talking therapies, ACT (Acceptance and Commitment Therapy) and CBT (Cognitive Behavioural Therapy).

His own methodology of change has evolved in tandem with his own journey from the prison cell to the boardroom.

Recognised for his strong leadership and communication skills he now supports leadership teams and coaches at all levels in organisations as they seek to implement change, both personal and corporate.

As a powerful, inspiring professional speaker he challenges individuals and teams to recognise their own potential and mind-traps, as well as their personal responsibility for making change.

Gethin has a unique combination of academic, professional and personal experience that enables him to "pick and mix" exactly what is required for organisational, team and individual change.

Change for the better isn't an academic exercise for him, but his mission.

www.synergy-sucess.net

Other dot dot dot publishing ●●● Titles

The Little Book of Holistic Accounting

Emma J Perry

ISBN–978-1-907282-81-2

For those stuck in a job or path that is stifling. How to balance the books of your body, mind, heart and soul.

Breathe with Ease

Alison Waring

ISBN– 978-1-907282-88-1

A powerful. natural approach to health. How to enable those with asthma and other breathing-related challenges to breathe with ease.

Lightning Source UK Ltd.
Milton Keynes UK
UKHW01f0935021018
329834UK00003B/40/P

9 781907 282867